5

Grant

Julia Dent Grant

Julia Dent Grant

★★★★★★★★★★★★★★★★★★★★★★

1826–1902

BY CHRISTINE A. FITZ-GERALD

CHILDREN'S PRESS®
A Division of Grolier Publishing
New York   London   Hong Kong   Sydney
Danbury, Connecticut

Consultants: TERRY J. MILLER
                      Site Manager, Galena State Historic Sites,
                      Illinois Historic Preservation Agency
                      LINDA CORNWELL
                      Learning Resource Consultant
                      Indiana Department of Education

Project Editor: DOWNING PUBLISHING SERVICES
Page Layout: CAROLE DESNOES
Photo Researcher: JAN IZZO

Visit Children's Press on the Internet at:
http://publishing.grolier.com

Library of Congress Cataloging-in-Publication Data

Fitz-Gerald, Christine Maloney.
      Julia Dent Grant / by Christine A. Fitz-Gerald.
         p. cm. — (Encyclopedia of First Ladies)
      Includes bibliographical references and index.
      Summary: A biography of the woman who spent much of her married life as an "army wife" before
becoming First Lady when her husband served as eighteenth president of the United States.
      ISBN 0-516-20696-6
      1. Grant, Julia Dent, 1826–1902—Juvenile literature.   2. Presidents' spouses—United States—
Biography—Juvenile literature.   3. Grant, Ulysses S. (Ulysses Simpson), 1822–1885—Juvenile literature.
[1. Grant, Julia Dent, 1826–1902.   2. First ladies.   3. Women—Biography.   4. Grant, Ulysses S.
(Ulysses Simpson), 1822–1885.]   I. Title.   II. Series.
E672.1.G3F58   1998   98-21383
973.8'2'092—dc21   CIP
[B]   AC

Table of Contents

Julia Dent Grant

CHAPTER ONE

Galena

Julia Dent Grant was eager for her husband, Ulysses S. Grant, to go to war in the spring of 1861. Certainly, she would miss him. The Grants shared a close, affectionate marriage. Her own political convictions had nothing to do with her desire to have him fight in the War Between the States. Julia was Southern by upbringing and in her sympathies. Ulysses, on the other hand, was determined to join the Northern army. Julia simply felt that Ulysses Grant was a great man and she did not intend to stand in the way of his destiny. Grant was grateful for her support. He wrote, "Julia takes a very sensible view of the present difficulties and will not throw a single obstacle in the way." She was not fearful for him. "My enthusiasm almost amounted to a delirium. I never once expected to hear bad news from my General. I do not know why. I knew—I felt—he would be victorious," she wrote.

At the outbreak of the American Civil War, the Grants were living in Galena, Illinois. They were newcomers to the town since they had lived there for only a year. So far, Ulysses Grant had not been a successful businessman. He had failed at both farming and business in Missouri. At the age of thirty-eight, he had brought his family to Illinois. There, he planned to sell leather goods such as saddles and bridles in his father's store. The store was part of his father's tannery business. Grant, who had never wanted to work in the family business, quietly resigned himself to being a leather merchant.

Galena, Illinois, as it looked about the time the Grants moved there

The Grants and their four children lived in this brick home in Galena.

Although Ulysses was unsatisfied at work, he was content with life at home. Julia Grant was gifted with a cheerful, optimistic nature. She created a home atmosphere that was relaxed and light-hearted. Economic hardship had not changed her happy personality or shaken her faith in her husband.

The Grants rented a small brick house in Galena. Julia and Ulysses lived there with their four children: Frederick, Ulysses, Ellen, and Jesse.

The daily routine of life was shattered by war. The American Civil War pitted two geographic regions of the United States against each other: the

11

Abraham Lincoln (1809–1865)

☆ ☆

Next to George Washington, Abraham Lincoln might be the most familiar American in history. Everyone recognizes his slightly sad face (it's on the $5 bill today); we celebrate his birthday (February 12); towns, companies, and cars bear his name. The well-known story of his childhood in a log cabin and his rise from poverty to become the sixteenth president of the United States has inspired generations of Americans. A natural storyteller, he had a sharp sense of humor and tremendous powers of concentration. Tall and gangly, Lincoln cast a long shadow even in his own time, leading the nation through the horror of the Civil War. He steadfastly supported General Grant in those years, finding in him the military leader the Union so badly needed. In return, Grant remembered President Lincoln as "a man of great ability, pure patriotism, unselfish nature" and predicted that his fame would grow over the years. Sadly, Abraham Lincoln was the first American president to be assassinated.

Crowds gathered on the housetops of Charleston to watch the Confederate attack on Fort Sumter, which started the Civil War on April 12, 1861.

North and the South. Each had very different economic interests. The North was largely industrial; the South was agrarian.

The South depended on slave labor to run its large plantations. There was strong antislavery feeling in the North. In the late 1850s, the Republican Party grew in strength. That party was committed to abolishing slavery. The Republican candidate, Abraham Lincoln, won the presidential campaign of 1860. The Southern states decided to secede from, or leave, the United States.

Eleven states seceded and set up their own government, the Confederate States of America. The Northern states (the Union) fought to bring the South back into the United States. The Southern states (the Confederacy) fought to be separate.

The Confederacy began the hostilities with an attack on Fort Sumter on

From West Point to War

✶ ✶

Ulysses S. Grant is among many famous graduates of the United States Military Academy at West Point, New York. One fellow cadet was Robert E. Lee, who graduated several years before Grant. Lee was the better student, graduating second in his class of 1829. Grant, who entered the academy ten years later, excelled only in horsemanship.

Neither Grant nor Lee knew they would face each other on the battlefields of the Civil War some twenty-five years later. They were not alone. Commanders on both sides in fifty-five major Civil War battles had trained at West Point.

April 12, 1861. President Lincoln called for 75,000 volunteers to join the Union army.

In Galena, a town meeting was held to discuss recruitment. Julia watched as a torchlight procession formed in the streets. She was afraid for her family and friends in the South, but she recognized that the war was an opportunity for her husband. "I did not think Captain Grant's occupation in Galena entirely congenial to him and was willing, therefore, that he should go out on this expedition as he wished, no matter how lonely I might be," she remembered.

Colonel Ulysses S. Grant went off to war with his horse, Rondy, and his eleven-year-old son, Fred.

Because of his military experience, Ulysses Grant was chosen by his townsmen to preside over the meeting. Grant was so energized by the thought of war that he immediately left the leather business. He wrote, "I never went into our leather store after that meeting, to put up a package or do other business."

For several months, Grant was frustrated in his attempts to enter the war as a colonel in the Union army. As a West Point graduate and a Mexican War army veteran, he was well qualified. Men with no military experience were receiving officer's commissions. Finally, in June 1861, Grant was made a colonel of the 21st Illinois Volunteers. Although he had not been the first choice, he was happy to be a colonel in charge of a regiment.

Julia began sewing his uniform. An officer had to have a horse, so the Grants borrowed money to buy one. When Grant was ready to leave Galena with his regiment, Julia had an unusual request. She asked her husband to take eleven-year-old Fred with him. Julia later remembered, "these regiments were only called out for three months, and I considered it a pleasant summer outing for both of them." Fred was eager to go and Ulysses was agreeable, so father and son rode off to war. Julia remained at home with the other three children.

CHAPTER TWO

White Haven

✶ ✶ ✶ ✶ ✶ ✶ ✶ ✶ ✶ ✶ ✶ ✶ ✶ ✶ ✶

The Dents were wealthy enough to own two homes. One was a house in St. Louis, Missouri. The other a farm that lay 10 miles (16 kilometers) west of the city. Of the two homes, Julia Dent far preferred the farm, which was called White Haven. She was born there on January 26, 1826, the fifth of the eight children of Frederick and Ellen Dent.

To Julia, city life could not equal the pleasures of life on the farm. Julia roamed the woods, fished, gardened, rode horses, and played with her brothers and sisters.

Julia admitted to being "something of a pet." Certainly, she was her father's favorite. Frederick Dent

✶ ✶ ✶ ✶ ✶ ✶ ✶ ✶ ✶ ✶ ✶ ✶ ✶ ✶ ✶

Portrait of America, 1826: The End of the Beginning

★ ★

As Julia Dent was born, two famous Americans died—Thomas Jefferson and John Adams, founding fathers of the American democracy. Both died on the fiftieth anniversary of the signing of the Declaration of Independence. It was the end of an era.

Born with Julia in 1826, however, was a new age of expansion and transportation. John Quincy Adams, son of the famous patriot, was then the sixth U.S. president. The country included 24 states; the edge of white settlement lay along the Mississippi River. Restless Americans, eager to explore the vast lands beyond, packed up their Conestoga wagons and headed west. Mountain men and fur trappers dared to cross the rugged Rocky Mountains. Americans loved to hear about the frontiersmen and their adventures. The most popular song of the day celebrated "The Hunters of Kentucky." The frontier also inspired America's first fictional hero, Natty Bumppo. In 1826, everyone was reading about his adventures in James Fenimore Cooper's book, *The Last of the Mohicans*.

How would Americans get around their growing country? The first railroads were built in 1826. Powered by horses, sails, or cables, they were called "short lines" because they covered small distances. Along the Erie Canal, goods, people, and ideas floated across upstate New York to the Great Lakes on barges towed by mules. Steamboats plied the rivers. "Corduroy roads" (planks laid parallel to keep wagon wheels out of the mud) crisscrossed the countryside. Americans on the move barely minded the bumpy ride.

Ten million people lived here in 1826. Of nearly two million African Americans, most lived as slaves in the South. Laborers from Germany and Ireland began to arrive in large numbers to work on the canals and railroads. Native Americans, to whom the "frontier" was home, moved west reluctantly, displaced by white settlers who wanted their lands.

The Dents' St. Louis house

and livestock. Julia remembered, "Papa found the place and the life so delightful that he gradually gave up all occupation and passed his time in the summer months sitting in an easy chair, reading an interesting book, and in the winter, in the chimney corner beside a blazing hickory fire, occupied in the same way."

Ellen Bray Wrenshall Dent had been born in England and educated in Philadelphia. Julia described her mother as kind and gentle but delicate in health. She enjoyed reading and music, and, unlike her husband and her eldest daughter, Ellen "hated the country and this place [White Haven], especially."

Julia attended a local, one-room schoolhouse until the age of ten. At that time, she was sent to boarding school in St. Louis. Julia admitted that she learned only subjects that she liked: history, mythology, and singing. Her teachers were frustrated by her refusal to learn mathematics and grammar.

At the age of seventeen, in the spring of 1844, Julia left school and returned to White Haven. In her

was not an affable man. He liked to argue, and he often started lawsuits over minor matters, but Julia had a way with him.

Originally from Maryland, Dent had made enough money as a merchant in Pittsburgh, Pennsylvania, and St. Louis to buy White Haven and retire. The Dents owned eighteen slaves who worked on White Haven. The farm had crops, orchards, gardens,

19

The One-Room Schoolhouse

✫ ✫

Rural children of young Julia's age usually attended a one-room schoolhouse. Students of all ages took classes together. In the center of the room, a wood-burning stove provided the only heat. The students sat on hard wooden benches and wrote on small slates. Lessons covered the basic skills of "reading, writing, and 'rithmetic," known as the three Rs. Geography and history were important, too, and manners were sometimes taught. The school year followed the patterns of farm life because children helped at home with chores and fieldwork. As a result, school terms generally ran about three months—from the fall harvest to the spring planting.

absence, the Dents had frequently entertained a young lieutenant named Ulysses S. Grant. Grant and Julia's brother Fred had been friends and roommates at West Point. Grant was now stationed at neighboring Jefferson Barracks. It was the largest military base in the United States and was located scarcely 5 miles (8 km) from White Haven. Grant had been visiting the Dents several times a week. After Julia's return, Grant found that his visits "certainly did become more enjoyable."

Ulysses Grant was born on April 27, 1822, in Point Pleasant, Ohio. He was the first child of Jesse and Hannah Grant. Physically, he was short and slender and had strong features. He was shy and given to long silences. Julia's enthusiasm and warmth attracted him immediately.

They had interests in common. From boyhood on, Grant had shown remarkable ability as a rider. Julia was an excellent horsewoman who loved the outdoors. She possessed energy and stamina enough to match Grant,

Missouri, U.S.A.

✶ ✶

Julia Dent was born in the country's newest state in 1826. When Missouri joined the Union in 1821 as the twenty-fourth state, St. Louis was a bustling city located on the edge of the western frontier. For many pioneers, St. Louis was the last outpost of civilization they would see before their long journey west. It also occupied the border between free states and slave states—between North and South. After much controversy, Missouri came into the Union as a slave state. By the time of the Civil War, Missouri almost left the Union with the other slave states. However, even though Missouri allowed slaveholding, it eventually sided with the Union. This created many divided loyalties, sometimes pitting brother against brother. Tensions between Julia's and Ulysses's families arose because of differing beliefs about slavery.

Ulysses S. Grant was born in this house in Point Pleasant, Ohio, on April 27, 1822.

Grant's parents, Hannah and Jesse R. Grant

who was a restless man. She did not mind his silences and he loved her conversation and stories.

Julia, at seventeen, was dark-haired and not quite 5 feet (150 centimeters) tall. She was not pretty and the muscles of her right eye caused it to move up and down involuntarily. None of this mattered to Grant, who found her attractive in every way.

One spring day, Julia and Ulysses were driving a carriage over a bridge that spanned a flooded creek. Julia announced to Ulysses that if the bridge were to collapse, she "would cling to him no matter what." He quickly asked her if she would like to cling to him forever.

In the summer, Ulysses's regiment was suddenly transferred to Louisiana. Julia had met Ulysses only three months earlier. Now she feared that she would never see him again. He was visiting his family in Georgetown, Ohio, and might have left for Louisiana from there.

Julia dreamed that Grant, dressed in civilian clothing, came to visit her. Julia believed in dreams and was reassured that she would see Ulysses again.

Meanwhile, Ulysses had asked for an extended leave in order to see Julia. Riding to White Haven, he swam his horse across a rain-swollen creek. Grant arrived at White Haven so drenched that one of Julia's brothers lent him dry clothes. Ulysses told Julia that he loved her, in what he later described as "the most awkward way

Ulysses Grant grew up in this house in Georgetown, Ohio. The house was built by his father shortly after the family moved to Georgetown in 1823.

The Mexican War: Fast Facts

WHAT: A war to acquire Mexican territory for the United States

WHEN: 1846–1848

WHO: Between the United States and Mexican armies

WHERE: Battles fought as far north as present-day Los Angeles and south to Mexico City

WHY: American president James Polk had been unable to purchase California and New Mexico from the Mexican government and decided to take them by force.

OUTCOME: In the Treaty of Guadalupe Hidalgo, Mexico gave the United States the land it wanted, which included southern California and most of the Southwest, in exchange for $15 million. Fifty thousand Mexican soldiers and thirteen thousand Americans died in the conflict.

imaginable." She admitted that she loved him but she doubted that her father would approve the match.

Grant went to Louisiana with no assurance that he would be able to marry Julia. He came north on leave to ask Frederick Dent for permission to marry Julia. Dent said that he could not bear the thought of Julia being married to a soldier, since military life was both dangerous and uncomfortable. Grudgingly, Dent agreed that if the couple still wished to marry after two years, he would not prevent them.

Two years stretched into four years. Ulysses Grant fought in the Mexican War, a war that he regarded as unjust and "unholy." It was, on the part of the United States, a blatant grab for territory. Grant observed, "We were sent to provoke a fight but it was essential that Mexico commence it." Grant absorbed a wealth of knowledge about war, battle, and leadership.

Julia used the years to work on her trousseau, the traditional collection of clothing and linens that brides brought to a marriage. She wrote to "her darling little lieutenant," although not often enough to satisfy him.

When Ulysses reappeared in the summer of 1848, Julia was elated. The couple married in a candlelit service in the Dent home in St. Louis on the evening of August 22, 1848. The bride was twenty-two years old, the groom twenty-six. The only somber note was the absence of Grant's family. They refused to attend because they objected to Ulysses's marriage into a slave-owning family.

CHAPTER THREE

Hardscrabble

☆ ☆ ☆ ☆ ☆ ☆ ☆ ☆ ☆ ☆ ☆ ☆ ☆ ☆ ☆ ☆

Julia adapted well to being a soldier's wife. She made friends quickly, both at Sackets Harbor, New York, and Detroit, Michigan. Money was tight but Julia managed to make their living quarters attractive.

Soon after arriving at Sackets Harbor, Julia panicked when Ulysses invited several officers to dinner. Ulysses was amazed at her reaction, since he had hired a cook. Julia insisted that they could not entertain guests until they were sure that their cook really could cook. Grant replied that he had thought all cooks could cook. Julia assured him that this was not so. Grant had to withdraw his invitations. After a trial

☆ ☆ ☆ ☆ ☆ ☆ ☆ ☆ ☆ ☆ ☆ ☆ ☆ ☆ ☆ ☆

An Angel in the House

✫ ✫

Women of Julia Grant's time faced a dilemma. Their mothers and grandmothers had worked side by side with husbands and sons to run family farms and shops. However, as industry replaced farming, men began to go off to work. Women stayed home raising families and tending to the household. Believing them responsible for the future of the nation, nineteenth-century Americans viewed this as a sacred duty. Women were held in high regard as keepers of the home. A wife and mother was expected to set high moral standards and live as an "angel in the house."

At the same time, however, women's rights by law and custom were extremely limited. Married women remained little more than the property of their husbands. They couldn't vote, own property, attend college, speak in public, or hold office. Although many women—widows, the poor, and free African Americans in particular—needed to work to support themselves, few jobs were available to them. Most of them worked as servants in other women's homes.

Conditions changed slowly. In 1848, when Julia was twenty-two, the women's rights movement began with a convention in upstate New York. For the next fifty years, Susan B. Anthony, Elizabeth Cady Stanton, and many other women worked tirelessly to achieve equal rights under the law for women.

Susan B. Anthony

meal, Julia proclaimed that the cook was adequate. The same officers were reinvited for dinner the next day.

In Detroit, Julia organized a masquerade ball. She attended as a tambourine girl. Ulysses wore his military uniform. He hated to dance and was content to watch Julia, who danced well.

In the spring of 1850, Julia returned to White Haven to give birth to her first child, Frederick, on May 30, 1850. Two years later, Julia traveled to the home of her in-laws in Bethel, Ohio, to give birth to a second son. Ulysses Simpson was born on July 22, 1852. The family always called this son Buck.

As Buck was being born, Ulysses Grant was crossing the Isthmus of Panama on a ship. He was on his way to a military post on the Pacific Coast. Julia's pregnancy prevented her from accompanying him.

Julia was uncomfortable staying with her in-laws. She felt that Grant's family, "with the exception of his mother, did not like me, which may, perhaps, have been my own fault; but we were brought up in different schools. They considered me unpardonably extravagant, and I considered them inexcusably the other way." She left Ohio and returned to White Haven with her sons.

Away from his family, Grant became despondent and bored with the tedious routine of military life. In the spring of 1854, he resigned from the army and came home.

Grant's immediate concern was supporting his family. Julia had received 60 acres (24 hectares) of wooded land from her father as a wedding gift, and the Grants decided to farm this land. They lived in a small cottage that had been loaned to them by Julia's brother Louis. Steadily, Ulysses cleared the timber from the land and chopped it into firewood. He carted it by the wagonload into St. Louis, where he sold it. Meanwhile, the Grant's third child, Ellen, called Nellie, was born on July 4, 1855. Julia cared for the children, grew vegetables, and raised chickens.

Neither Julia nor Ulysses wished to depend on family members for assistance. They built a log cabin and left the loaned cottage to move into it.

Nellie Grant at the age of three

The Grants called their new home Hardscrabble.

Difficult times followed as Julia and Ulysses toiled to make a success of farming. There was little time for amusement and even less money. In 1857, all the crops failed. Julia's mother died in July of that year. Ulysses became ill. He suffered from fevers and severe coughing for an entire year. Julia, who was usually cheerful and optimistic, later admitted that she felt despondent at times during the Hardscrabble days. The Grant's fourth child, Jesse, was born in February 1858.

By autumn 1858, the Grants were ready to quit farming and try something else. Ulysses joined Julia's cousin, Harry Boggs, in a real estate business in St. Louis. The Grants rented a small house in the city. There were so many real estate firms in St. Louis that the competition for business was fierce. Ulysses Grant was far too reserved and quiet to be successful in this setting.

As the real estate business foundered, the friendship between the Grants and the Boggs began to unravel. Julia was aware that Ulysses was so sympathetic to renters that he often failed to collect the rents on time. The real estate partnership crumpled in 1859. Ulysses's father, Jesse Grant,

Hardscrabble, the log cabin built by Grant in 1855 near St. Louis

offered his son a job in the family business, working in a leather store in Galena, Illinois.

Before leaving Missouri, Ulysses Grant freed his only slave, William. He could have sold William for a thousand dollars but had come to feel that slavery was wrong. Julia herself owned four slaves—Eliza, Dan, Julia, and John. She could not take them to Illinois, which was a free state. Instead, she rented their services to other families living in Missouri.

In April 1860, the Grants arrived

31

Before 1860, when the Grants arrived, Galena (above) had been a boomtown thanks to the lead mines and heavy traffic on the Mississippi River.

in Galena. Thirty years earlier, Galena had been a boomtown because of its lead mines and river traffic. The town had since been overtaken in importance by Chicago. Nevertheless, Galena still had a number of thriving businesses. Julia hoped that her family would find prosperity in Galena.

Inventing America

★ ★

New inventions enter our lives every day. We have grown used to millions of products that make our work, travel, and communication easier and our play more fun. This inventive spirit really began during Julia Grant's lifetime, more than a hundred years ago. Take a look at a handful of the discoveries people made during this period, which was called the Industrial Revolution: the steam locomotive, perfected by Peter Cooper in 1830, made transportation faster; the reaper, invented by Cyrus McCormick in 1831, made farming more efficient; the telegraph, invented by Samuel F. B. Morse in 1844, made communication easier; the passenger elevator, invented by Elisha Otis in 1853, made tall buildings possible. Throughout her lifetime, Julia saw the horsedrawn, handmade, homespun way of life give way to industry and invention.

The Best Friend of Charleston *was the first steam locomotive put into regular service in the United States. It began operating in Charleston, South Carolina, on Christmas Day, 1830.*

★ ★ ★ ★ ★ ★ ★ ★ ★ ★ ★ ★ ★ ★ ★ ★

CHAPTER FOUR

Civil War

✯ ✯ ✯ ✯ ✯ ✯ ✯ ✯ ✯ ✯ ✯ ✯ ✯ ✯ ✯ ✯

When the American Civil War erupted in 1861, many men rushed to enlist in the army. Women, faced with the absence of husbands and sons, assumed increased responsibilities. Julia longed to be involved in the war effort. She attended a sewing meeting, at which she was asked to knit socks for the soldiers. "I had to confess . . . that I did not even know how to begin them and that I feared the war would be over before I possibly could finish them," she wrote.

Julia never attended another sewing meeting. She soon found that caring for her family in Ulysses's absence was very demanding. Fred was back in Galena

✯ ✯ ✯ ✯ ✯ ✯ ✯ ✯ ✯ ✯ ✯ ✯ ✯ ✯ ✯ ✯

The Civil War: Fast Facts

WHAT: The War Between the States

WHEN: 1861–1865

WHO: Between the Union (Northern states) and the Confederacy (Southern states)

WHERE: Battles fought as far north as Pennsylvania, south to Florida, and west into Missouri

WHY: Many complicated reasons contributed to the outbreak of civil war. Basic differences between the economies and ways of life in the North and the South led to disagreements over slavery and the power of states versus the federal government. When the Southern states left the Union to form their own government, war soon followed.

OUTCOME: After a devastating loss of American life, Northern and Southern, the Union won the war largely because the South ran out of supplies, men, and energy. Slavery was abolished, and the Confederate states returned to the Union.

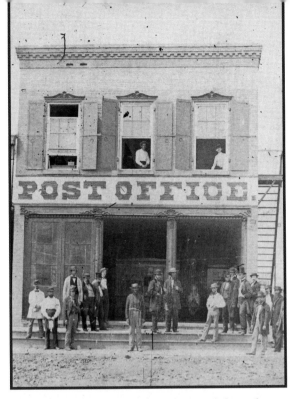

General Grant (*standing at center with his right hand in his pocket*) *at his headquarters below the post office at Cairo, Illinois, in September 1861*

by July. His father sent him home when he knew that his regiment was going into battle.

Julia pored over her husband's letters and followed the war news in the newspaper. Newspaper correspondents accompanied the troops during the Civil War, so coverage was good. In August, the newspaper announced that Ulysses Grant had been promoted to general.

Grant missed Julia and the children and asked her to visit him at his headquarters in Cairo, Illinois. She stalled because "it was such an undertaking to go with four children." In

Women and the War

☆ ☆

Women contributed in many ways to the war effort. In both the North and the South, they gathered funds, medical supplies, and clothing for the soldiers. Some women used the opportunity to take the jobs and run the farms that the men had left. On the battlefields, women served as nurses, although they were not encouraged to do so. A handful of women, disguised as men, fought on the front lines for what they believed. As women's roles changed during the Civil War, they learned about independence, self-reliance, and organization. After the war, many women used their new skills to seek equality for themselves.

November 1861, she made the trip and found that she enjoyed it.

This was only the first of her many trips to be with Grant during the war. Sometimes she brought the children; sometimes she came alone. Grant loved to have her near him. Julia was always cheerful and encouraging. She never complained about the discomforts of life at the front. She nursed Grant through his frequent migraine headaches. Grant's staff came to admire her and accept her presence. After Julia began to care for the wounded men in the field hospital, Grant begged her to let others help the wounded. He said, "I hear of these all day long and I sent for you to come that I might have a little rest from all this sad part. I do not want you to know about these things. I want you to tell me of the children and yourself. I want and need a little rest and sunshine."

This photograph was taken of General Grant and his staff at the front. Grant is at left center, leaning against a tree with a document in his right hand.

At the Battle of Shiloh on April 6–7, 1862, General Grant held off a Confederate attack and forced the Southern soldiers to retreat. Though Grant won the battle, thousands of Northern and Southern troops died.

By now, it was apparent that the war would not be over quickly. Julia was unsure where she and the children should live while Ulysses was gone. When she visited her father in St. Louis, she felt tense and unhappy. Frederick Dent was furious at his son-in-law for fighting for the Union. Many of Julia's old friends, neighbors, and relatives supported the Confederacy and openly criticized Julia's husband.

Although she had never been at ease with the Grant family, she did live with them for long periods during the war so that her children could attend school regularly.

Julia was hurt whenever Ulysses Grant was criticized in the newspapers. After the bloody Battle of Shiloh, the newspapers portrayed Grant as a drunken, incompetent butcher. Julia remembered, "I sat shocked and almost stunned at an

39

Robert E. Lee (1807–1870)

☆ ☆

In 1861, Robert E. Lee was offered command of the Union armies. Although he opposed slavery, he refused the appointment, wishing to remain loyal to his native Virginia. Lee's loyalty, sense of duty, and dignity won him respect throughout his life. After the Civil War, the general became president of Washington College in Lexington, Virginia. He believed the future of the South lay in its youth. He preached gentlemanly behavior, peaceable reunion with the North, and hard work. Students from both the North and the South flocked to the school to learn from him.

article (many of them) in ribald abuse of my husband, just after the Battle of Shiloh."

In truth, Grant was a gifted general. He was determined and decisive. Although he himself was a kindhearted man, he understood that war was about killing and he never balked at the fact. His willingness to accept high casualties as the price of victory made him a very controversial figure.

Ulysses S. Grant and Robert E. Lee were the two greatest generals of the Civil War. Lee's brilliant leadership was well recognized before the war began, but Grant entered the war in obscurity. His rise to fame may have been predictable to Julia, but it surprised nearly everyone else.

The Civil War was fought in two theaters, or areas. In the East, the Confederate army of Northern Virginia, led by Robert E. Lee, opposed the Union army of the Potomac. Most of the fighting was in Virginia, Maryland, and Pennsylvania. For the first three years of the war, the Union army of the Potomac lost battles because of a lack of effective leadership.

It was a different story in the West, where Union forces won battles early in the war, not least because of the leadership of Ulysses Grant. The fighting occurred along the Mississippi River and in Tennessee and northern Georgia.

Grant's first major victory, the capture of Fort Donelson in February 1862, earned him the nickname "Unconditional Surrender Grant." He won a bloody victory at Pittsburg Landing, Tennessee, in April 1862. This battle was named Shiloh for the wooden church that stood on the battlefield. Shiloh could easily have been a major defeat for the Union troops,

Johnny Reb and Billy Yank

✦ ✦

At the beginning of the Civil War, farmers, craftsmen, businessmen, and laborers rushed to enlist in the armies of both the North and the South. Nearly 3 million soldiers served in the war. Among Northern troops, 190,000 were African American. Most troops were between the ages of seventeen and twenty-five, but drummer boys as young as twelve signed up as well. It didn't take long for the glory of war to turn bitter. Soldiers lived in crowded tent cities when they weren't fighting, marching, or digging trenches. Fierce and deadly battles interrupted weeks of boredom and loneliness. A lack of fresh water and a diet of hardtack (a hard biscuit) and beans led to so much sickness that twice as many men died of disease as from enemy fire. By the end of the war, nearly 620,000 Americans had perished.

who were surprised by a Confederate attack. Instead, Grant managed to turn the two-day battle into a victory. Three thousand men were killed at Shiloh. Grant was blamed for the heavy losses. Abraham Lincoln defended him, stating, "I can't spare this man. He fights."

As Grant became better known, Julia was often recognized as the general's wife. Confederate troops were aware that she often traveled to Grant's headquarters. Julia was almost captured by Confederate soldiers in December 1862 in Holly Springs, Mississippi.

Vast stores of food, guns, and ammunition were being stockpiled in Holly Springs. The Union would need these supplies for an attack on Vicksburg, Mississippi, which was a Confederate stronghold. Julia was staying in a Holly Springs mansion belonging to a Confederate family named Walters. The Walters were courteous but cold to Julia. When the Confederate cavalry stormed into Holly Springs, the Union forces were surprised and overwhelmed. The troopers plundered the Union sup-

plies. They took whatever they could carry and burned the rest. The Confederate troopers went to the Walters' house, looking for Julia. Luckily, she had left town before the attack. She was with Grant in nearby Oxford, Mississippi. The Walters refused to give the soldiers any of Julia's personal belongings. Her horses were taken, however, and her carriage was destroyed. It had been a close call for Julia.

Julia remained in Mississippi to watch Union gunboats try to reach Vicksburg in April 1863. Grant's army had been bogged down in swampy land across the Mississippi River from Vicksburg. Grant had decided to ferry his troops across the Mississippi and land them south of Vicksburg. It was a gamble because it put the army, as Grant wrote, "in the enemy's country with a vast river between me and my base of supplies." The boats carrying the Union army had to pass by the powerful gun batteries that guarded Vicksburg. Julia observed the manuever from aboard a steamship. It was nighttime and she remembered that "all was going well when a red glare

These Union ships carrying Grant's troops managed to reach safety south of Vicksburg in April 1863, even though powerful gun batteries guarded the town.

flashed up from the Vicksburg shore and the flotilla of gunboats and transport and our own boats were made plainly visible." Despite heavy bombardment, the Union ships reached safety.

Julia returned to St. Louis before Vicksburg surrendered on July 4, 1863. Fred, however, was with his father during the entire seige. He was wounded slightly in the leg and he contracted dysentery. He returned to St. Louis just as Julia was about to depart again to visit her husband. Julia admitted, "I did not realize how ill he was or I should not have left him."

In December, Julia received a telegram that Fred was very ill with

Lieutenant General Ulysses S. Grant and his family posed for this photograph at the time President Lincoln promoted Grant to general-in-chief of all the Union armies in March 1864.

pneumonia. She left Grant's headquarters in Nashville, Tennessee, and returned to St. Louis to nurse Fred. By January, it appeared that Fred was dying. Julia sent for Ulysses, but by the time he arrived, Fred had passed through the worst of his illness and was recovering.

Soon after Fred's recovery, Ulysses

Grant was summoned to Washington by President Abraham Lincoln. Lincoln had been desperately seeking an effective general to lead the Union armies in the East. He had already promoted and then discarded six generals in rapid succession. None had brought the victories the Union needed. Lincoln now was convinced that he had found the right general for the job.

Ulysses Grant was promoted to general-in-chief of all the Union armies in March 1864. He was second in power only to the president himself. Grant traveled to Washington, with Fred, to receive the commission. Julia remained in Nashville.

Julia enjoyed the attention she received as the wife of a famous general.

General Grant at the time he was promoted to general-in-chief by President Abraham Lincoln

Julia was delighted but hardly surprised. She felt that her husband deserved this promotion. It was merely his due. Grant was becoming a famous man, and Julia was enjoying the attention she received as his wife. Grant's name was being mentioned in the newspapers as a probable presidential candidate in the next election. Although neither of the Grants realized it at the time, they would never again be obscure or unknown.

CHAPTER FIVE

Aftermath of War

☆ ☆ ☆ ☆ ☆ ☆ ☆ ☆ ☆ ☆ ☆ ☆ ☆ ☆ ☆ ☆

Grant proved to be the general Lincoln needed. He pursued Lee's army mercilessly in the last year of the Civil War. Lee's army was weakened by continuous fighting, and Grant kept pressing battle in an effort to force the end of the war. In the late spring of 1864, the armies fought a series of bloody battles at Wilderness, Spotsylvania, and Cold Harbor. Casualties were high on both sides but—as Grant well knew—the North, with its larger population, could absorb more losses than the South.

Julia had settled the family into a house in Burlington, New Jersey. She had chosen the town for

☆ ☆ ☆ ☆ ☆ ☆ ☆ ☆ ☆ ☆ ☆ ☆ ☆ ☆ ☆ ☆

This photograph of General Grant shows him in front of his tent headquarters after the Battle of Cold Harbor in the late spring of 1864.

cabin consisted of one large front room and two small back bedrooms.

President Lincoln frequently visited City Point with his wife, Mary Todd Lincoln. Mary Lincoln disliked Ulysses Grant and made no effort to be friendly to Julia. Nevertheless, Julia and Mary Lincoln were often thrown into each other's company.

At City Point, the Grants had the exclusive use of a boat called the *Mary Martin*. The presidential boat was the *River Queen*. Once, Mary Lincoln gave a party aboard the *River Queen* and did not invite Julia. Julia proceeded to take the only military band with her for an afternoon outing aboard the *Mary Martin*. Mary Lincoln was shocked to discover that there would be no music at her party because Julia had left with the band. As the *Mary Martin* passed the *River Queen*, Julia asked the band to play a tune called "Now You'll Remember Me."

In April 1865, a Union officer boarded the *Mary Martin* with a message for Julia. Lee had surrendered to Grant at Appomattox Court House, Virginia, on April 9. The Confederate army had been fleeing west, with the

its good schools. She was often at Grant's headquarters at City Point, Virginia. City Point was a military town of log cabins and tents, built on a hill above the James River. Grant's

Mary Todd Lincoln (1818–1882)

★ ★

In her youth, Mary Todd was the belle of frontier Illinois. While living with her sister and brother-in-law in Springfield, she met and fell in love with a young lawyer named Abraham Lincoln. After a tumultuous and partly secret courtship, the two were married in her sister's home. Mary predicted that Abraham would be president. When he was elected in 1860, she became an outspoken First Lady, at times addressing Congress. The sad deaths of her sons and husband brought on a lasting mental illness. After a short term in an asylum, she traveled and lived abroad but was forced to return home when she injured her spine. She died in the house where she had married Abraham Lincoln.

Union army in pursuit. Although many of Lee's men were ill and starving, Lee intended to turn and fight. Then he realized that his army was encircled by Union troops. Knowing that resistance would be a pointless sacrifice of lives, he chose to surrender.

Lee rode to meet Grant in a new uniform. His boots were polished to a high sheen. His spurs were golden and he carried a bejeweled sword, which he expected to relinquish to Grant. Grant, who was recovering from a migraine headache, wore a dusty, unpressed uniform. His coat

President Abraham Lincoln met with his military staff to discuss terms of peace at the conclusion of the Civil War. General Grant is second from left.

was unbuttoned and he was swordless. His appearance was hardly elegant, but he distinguished himself by offering the beaten Confederate army generous terms of surrender. The Confederate soldiers were allowed to keep their personal weapons and goods. At Lee's request, Grant allowed the Confederate soldiers to take their horses with them, since they would need horses to plant crops. Grant did not ask Lee to surrender his beautiful sword, as was customary. Finally, Grant sent food rations to the starving Confederate army.

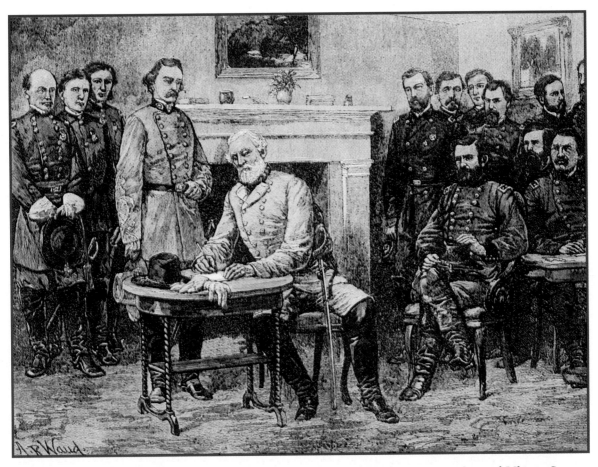

General Robert E. Lee (seated at table) surrendered the main Confederate army to General Ulysses S. Grant (seated with crossed legs) at Appomattox Court House, Virginia, on April 9, 1865.

The war was over. More than 600,000 men had died. The South was a devastated land in which cities, towns, farms, and plantations lay in ruins. Slavery was over in the South.

Julia and Ulysses Grant were in Washington, D.C., on April 13. The following day, the Grants were invited by the Lincolns to go to an evening performance of *Our American Cousin* at Ford's Theatre. Although Julia loved the theater, she declined the invitation, insisting that she and Ulysses must go home to see Fred, Buck, and Nellie. "As soon as I received the invitation to go with

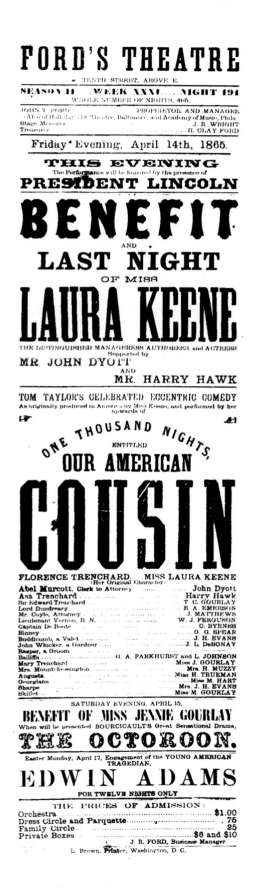

Mrs. Lincoln, I dispatched a note to General Grant entreating him to go home that evening . . . he must take me home . . . I do not know what possessed me to take such a freak but go home I felt I must," Julia recalled.

While Ulysses went to the White House to see President Lincoln, Julia and Jesse had lunch with friends at the Willard Hotel. Their meal was made uncomfortable by the strange behavior of a man at a nearby table. He stared at Julia and eavesdropped on her conversation. Later that day, as Julia, Ulysses, and Jesse were riding in a carriage to the train station, the same man, now on horseback, passed them and peered into their carriage. He swung around and returned to pass them again, staring at Ulysses Grant in a hostile way.

The Grants boarded a train for Burlington, New Jersey. When they stopped to dine at a hotel in Philadelphia, they were met by a mes-

This handbill advertised the play being performed at Ford's Theatre on the evening of April 14, 1865, when President Abraham Lincoln was shot.

The shooting of President Lincoln took place during a performance at Ford's Theatre. The Grants would have been in the president's box if they had accepted the Lincolns' invitation to join them that evening.

senger who had grim news. Abraham Lincoln had been shot at Ford's Theatre. He could not survive his wounds. The Grants would have been in the theater box with the Lincolns had Julia not refused to attend.

Abraham Lincoln died early in the morning of April 15, 1865. Before noon, Vice President Andrew Johnson was sworn in as president.

Several years later, Grant received an anonymous letter from a man who claimed to have been a member of the group that assassinated Lincoln. He wrote that he had followed the Grants from Washington to Philadelphia on

John Wilkes Booth (1838–1865)

☆ ☆

Born into a family of famous actors, young John Wilkes Booth spent little time in school. He eventually became a Shakespearean actor and made his debut in Baltimore at the age of seventeen. The most important role of his life came at Ford's Theatre, where on April 14, 1865, he sneaked into the presidential box and shot President Lincoln. Then he leaped to the stage crying, "The South is avenged!" and disappeared through the rear of the theater. He broke a leg during his getaway. Booth escaped on horseback and hid in a barn near Bowling Green, Virginia. After twelve days, he was found and died of gunshot wounds. No one is sure whether he shot himself or was killed by his captors.

Andrew Johnson (1808–1875)

☆ ☆

After Lincoln's death, the Radical Republicans who controlled Congress wanted to punish the South for fighting the Civil War. President Johnson wanted to "extend his hand" to the Southern states and bring them back into the Union as peaceably as possible. One of the laws Congress passed made it illegal for the president to fire anyone without congressional approval. This was clearly against the Constitution. When President Johnson fired a Radical Republican member of his Cabinet, Congress impeached him for breaking this law and put him on trial, hoping to remove him from the presidency. He was found not guilty and earned the title "Defender of the Constitution."

the day Lincoln was shot. He intended to kill Grant but failed because a train porter had locked the door on the Grants' private car. The man was relieved to have been prevented from committing a murder. Julia believed that the thin, intense man who had stared at her at the Willard Hotel, and later passed their carriage, was John Wilkes Booth, Lincoln's assassin.

The new president, Andrew Johnson, was a Southerner from Tennessee.

55

Johnson, however, had always supported the Union. The overwhelming issue of his presidency was how to restore the South to the Union. Johnson favored a merciful and generous approach to the "reconstruction" of the South. He merely wanted the Southern states to agree to abolish slavery and take an oath of loyalty to the United States. He was opposed by Radical Republicans, who wished to punish the South for the war. As the majority in Congress, the Radical Republicans were able to pass many harsh reconstruction bills.

Congress established martial law in the South, treating the defeated states like conquered enemies. Many Southern white men were barred from voting and holding any government office. Unscrupulous Northern politicians moved to the South to profit from the situation. They were known as "carpetbaggers" because they arrived with their possessions packed in a carpetbag. The South, already poor and in

Reconstruction

✲ ✲

Reconstruction came after the Civil War and was a time of great conflict. The Southern states were nearly destroyed by the fighting, and they had to "reconstruct" their lives from scratch. They also had to re-enter the Union. But rebuilding homes, cities, and farms would be much easier than rebuilding the South's relationship with the rest of the Union. It was especially hard for Southern blacks. Congress established the Freedmen's Bureau to provide food, clothing, shelter, and jobs for newly freed slaves. The bureau also set up hospitals and schools. However, without any land of their own to farm, blacks depended on white landowners for employment. Whites used this power to keep them out of politics and make them second-class citizens.

The Thirteenth Amendment

★ ★ ★ ★ ★ ★ ★ ★ ★ ★ ★ ★ ★ ★ ★ ★ ★ ★ ★

This short but powerful amendment to the U.S. Constitution became law in 1865:

"Neither slavery nor involuntary servitude . . . shall exist within the United States. . . ."

It ended nearly 250 years of bondage for African Americans, who had been enslaved as early as 1619 to work tobacco farms in the South. The abolition of slavery changed Southern life forever. The huge plantations failed because they could not run without slave labor. With their economy in ruins, white people became frustrated and angry. At the same time, black people, having won their freedom, set off down the difficult road to equality.

ruins, was further embittered by the harsh laws passed by Congress.

The Thirteenth Amendment to the Constitution was ratified in 1865, during Johnson's term. The amendment abolished slavery in the United States. Shortly before leaving office, Johnson declared a general amnesty for those who had fought against the Union.

★ ★ ★ ★ ★ ★ ★ ★ ★ ★ ★ ★ ★ ★ ★

CHAPTER SIX

The White House

✶ ✶ ✶ ✶ ✶ ✶ ✶ ✶ ✶ ✶ ✶ ✶ ✶ ✶ ✶

Julia and Ulysses Grant were seldom in one place for long between 1865 and 1869. They had a choice of residences: a home in Galena and a mansion in Philadelphia, both of which had been gifts. They also maintained a home in Washington, D.C.

Ulysses Grant had become an immensely popular national figure. It seemed inevitable that he would be the next president. No one was surprised when he received the Republican nomination. He had neither intense political convictions nor any specific goals for the nation; he won the election because of his military fame. Grant was inaugurated on March 4, 1869.

✶ ✶ ✶ ✶ ✶ ✶ ✶ ✶ ✶ ✶ ✶ ✶ ✶ ✶ ✶

This house in Galena was given to the Grants by the townspeople after the Civil War.

The Grant family leaving Galena for Washington, D.C., on November 7, 1868, after Grant's election as president

A portrait of Ulysses S. Grant as president

The Green Room was one of the many White House rooms decorated by Julia Grant while she was First Lady from 1869 to 1877.

At Home in the White House

☆ ☆

Julia loved the "dear old" White House, even though she was reluctant to move in at first. Years of neglect during the war had taken their toll on the mansion. The ceilings were cracked and falling, walls were damp, and wood was rotting. Fretting about the "widely scattered" furniture and the "worn and ugly" carpets, Julia began redecorating, reupholstering, and rearranging. By the time of Nellie's wedding in 1874, the Grants had transformed the White House into a glittering palace with sparkling chandeliers, elaborate ornamentation, soaring pillars, and elegant furniture. Some people thought that the decorating was overdone, but Washington society delighted in the extravagance of the Grants.

Julia was First Lady for eight years, from 1869 to 1877. She oversaw the renovation and redecoration of much of the White House. Some of the White House staff had become used to smoking in the lobby and eating lunch in a reception room. Julia put an end to that. She also insisted that staff members wear uniforms and gloves. Julia held a weekly reception in the Blue Room. With the assistance of Cabinet officers' wives, she greeted all visitors.

Once a week, the Grants gave opulent dinners for thirty-six. Julia hired an Italian chef named Melah to improve the food at the White House. Melah produced extravagant meals that sometimes included as many as thirty courses.

At the same time, Julia managed to maintain a warm, informal family life that was in sharp contrast to the glittering public parties and dinners. Ulysses and Julia always had breakfast together. On evenings when there was no official dinner or party, the Grants ate with their children. Much of the time, only Nellie and Jesse were there. Fred was a cadet at West Point and

A view of the White House as it looked during the Grant years, from 1869 to 1877

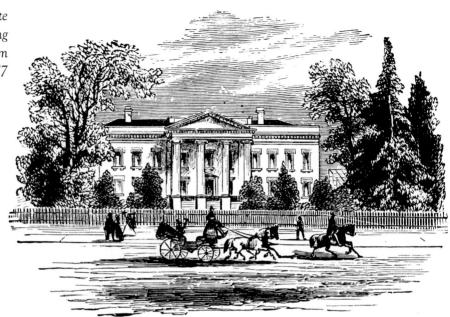

This dinner plate was part of the Grant's White House china.

Julia Grant wore this silver damask gown when she was First Lady.

The Grant family at their house in Long Branch. From left: Henry, the butler; Julia; Ulysses; Nellie; Ferdinand, the valet; Jesse; Jesse's friend Willie Coles; and U. S. Grant, Jr. (Buck)

Buck was studying at Harvard University. The Grants had sent Nellie to boarding school in Connecticut, but when she complained of homesickness in a matter of weeks, they brought her home. Jesse had an equally short stay at a boarding school near Philadelphia. He, like Nellie, pleaded homesickness and was allowed to return home.

The Grants escaped the hot, steamy summers in the capital by moving to their house in Long Branch, a beach resort on the New Jersey shore. They owned a roomy house with a large back porch and a private beach.

As First Lady, Julia was under public scrutiny. She had always been self-

The Grant's summer house in Long Branch, on the New Jersey shore

Developing Pictures

✫ ✫

In the middle of the eighteenth century, a wonderful new process became available to Americans: photography. For the first time, people could see actual pictures of presidents and first ladies, of kings and generals, and of each other. By 1850, everyone wanted to have a picture taken, and photography studios did a booming business. Posing for a portrait was uncomfortable, however, because the sitter had to keep perfectly still so the image wouldn't be blurred. Photographers steadied their subjects with metal neck braces cleverly hidden from the camera's eye. The Civil War was the first major event to be recorded in photographs. Hauling their heavy equipment around the battlefields in wagons, photographers produced mournful images of fallen soldiers to give Americans their first realistic glimpse of the horror of war.

A portrait of Nellie Grant as a bride

The newly redecorated East Room was the setting for Nellie Grant's wedding in May 1874.

conscious about her right eye. For photographs, she sat in profile rather than face the camera. She decided to have surgery to correct her eye problem but Ulysses talked her out of it. "This operation might make you look better to other people, but to me you are prettier as you are—as you were when I first saw you," he told her. Julia was relieved and canceled the surgery.

In May 1874, Nellie Grant married Algernon Charles Frederic Sartoris (pronounced SAHR-TRESS), in a lavish wedding held in the East Room of the White House. Nellie was eighteen years old and Sartoris was twenty-three. The couple had met aboard a ship when Nellie was returning home from a European tour. Sartoris was a handsome, wealthy Englishman. His

Ida Marie Honore married the Grant's oldest son, Frederick, in 1874.

father had been a member of the British Parliament. His maternal aunt was the famous British actress Fanny Kemble.

Appearances aside, Sartoris was hardly a splendid match. Sartoris's own parents wrote to the Grants to express their doubts about the wisdom of this marriage. They admitted that their son had a drinking problem and could be very difficult. Nellie, however, was determined to marry Sartoris.

The East Room was fragrant with thousands of flowers. The Marine band played for the occasion and a sumptuous wedding breakfast for the two hundred guests was served in the State Dining Room. Julia wore a dark silk dress because she was still in mourning for her father, who had died in 1873. Both Julia and Ulysses had tears in their eyes during the ceremony. Ulysses Grant disappeared after the wedding for a time and was found, weeping, in Nellie's old room. Julia was sad that her daughter would be living in England, so far away from home. A happier occasion was Fred's marriage, also in 1874, to Chicagoan Ida Marie Honore.

The political record of both Grant administrations was marred by corruption. Grant filled his Cabinet with former soldier friends and wealthy businessmen. Few of his political appointees were picked for their knowledge and experience. President Grant himself was honest, but many of the men he put in positions of power were dishonest and greedy. Worse yet, Grant continued to support the men he had chosen, even after some of them were caught in illegal dealings.

Grant also appointed many rela-

President Grant's Cabinet (above) was filled with friends from the military and wealthy businessmen.

tives, both Grants and Dents, to political office. This practice, called nepotism, was criticized in the press.

Following the Civil War, there had been a surge of economic growth in the North. Vast fortunes were made. The Grants became friendly with a number of wealthy, powerful men. Both Ulysses and Julia took many large and expensive presents, including houses, from their new friends.

They seemed not to understand that accepting those gifts gave the impression that they were taking bribes and put them in the position of owing political favors.

A great national achievement of the Grant years was the completion of a transcontinental railroad on May 10, 1869. One line had started in California and the other at the Mississippi River. The tracks met at Pro-

From Sea to Shining Sea

★ ★

At the end of the Civil War, railroads extended only as far west as Omaha, Nebraska. As the population of the West grew, the time came to connect California with the East Coast. The transcontinental railroad, begun in 1866, was a tremendous feat of construction accomplished largely by Chinese and Irish immigrants. The Irish built one line west from Omaha; the Chinese built the other line east from California. Through snowy mountains, over deep canyons, and across dusty plains, workers raced to connect the two lines in Utah. Crews on the Union Pacific line covered nearly 1,000 miles (1,609 kilometers) in three years. The workers on the Central Pacific line from California set the record. They laid 10 miles (16 km) of track in one day, an effort that involved driving 120,000 spikes into 31,000 ties!

A golden spike driven at Promontory Point, Utah, on May 10, 1869, marked the completion of the transcontinental railroad.

montory Point, Utah. A golden spike was driven to connect the railways.

The railroad spurred western expansion. When gold was discovered in the Black Hills of South Dakota, General George Armstrong Custer enthusiastically accepted the assignment of removing the Sioux Indians from that land. The Indians resisted. In June 1876, Custer and his men were overwhelmed and killed at the Battle of the Little Bighorn. Fred Grant was

George Armstrong Custer (1839–1876)

★ ★

Even though he graduated last in his class at West Point, this dashing young soldier became known for his daring in battle. In the last days of the Civil War, Custer kept the heat on Confederate troops, contributing to General Lee's decision to surrender. Custer was appointed lieutenant colonel of the Seventh Cavalry after the war. He led his troops out West to campaign against the Indians. Cavalrymen called him "Old Curly" and Indians knew him as "Long Hair the Woman Killer" because of his flowing blond locks. Custer believed he was indestructible, but the Sioux at the Little Bighorn proved him wrong.

one of Custer's officers. He would have been at the Little Bighorn had he not been on leave because his wife, Ida, was expecting a baby.

In 1868, the Ku Klux Klan was formed. Klansmen terrorized black people to keep them from voting. In response to the violence of the Klan, the Fifteenth Amendment to the Constitution was ratified in 1870. The amendment protected the voting rights of black people.

Julia had remained aloof from politics during her husband's two terms. Women were not allowed to vote. They were neither expected to be active in politics nor to even state a political opinion. Julia had enjoyed her social role as a White House hostess and she had become accustomed to power. She wanted Ulysses to run for a third term even though he had no desire to do so. Grant knew that the voters were disillusioned with him

Terrorism: Nothing New

✫ ✫

In the years after the Civil War, the South was in turmoil. Its buildings lay in ruins, and 300,000 of its young men had died in battle. At the same time, newly freed slaves sought to make a living, to vote, and to behave like U.S. citizens. Many white people felt threatened by the ending of life as they had known it and took up arms against blacks and those who supported their rights. One radical group of whites organized the Ku Klux Klan, a secret terrorist society. Riding at night—dressed as the ghosts of Confederate soldiers—klansmen frightened, beat, and murdered African Americans to keep them from voting. So violent were their actions that in 1870 and 1871 Congress passed several anti-Klan laws to forbid anyone from interfering with another's civil and political rights.

President Grant signed the Ku Klux Klan Act, a bill designed to enforce the Fourteenth Amendment (civil rights), on April 20, 1870. He later signed so-called force bills to enforce the Fifteenth Amendment.

because of the scandals and corruption within his administration. He was tired of the responsibility of being president, but he knew that Julia would try to talk him into running for a third term. Without telling her, he informed the newspapers that he would not seek reelection. Julia was hurt at not being consulted.

Rutherford B. Hayes won the presidential election of 1876. The Grants turned over the White House to the

Rutherford B. Hayes (1822–1893)

★ ★

The nineteenth president of the United States was elected by a single vote! His opponent, Democrat Samuel J. Tilden, appeared to have won the 1876 election. The Republicans challenged the vote counts from South Carolina, Louisiana, Florida, and Oregon. An Electoral Commission was formed to decide who would get the votes from these states. As it turned out, the Commission had one more Republican than Democrat. The votes were given to Hayes and he won. Behind the scenes, Southern Democrats agreed to accept this outcome only if all federal troops would leave South Carolina and Louisiana. This withdrawal signaled the end of Reconstruction.

incoming First Family and departed Washington by train. Leaving had been difficult for Julia. As the train pulled out of the station, she wept, "I feel like a waif, like a waif on the world's wide common."

★ ★ ★ ★ ★ ★ ★ ★ ★ ★ ★ ★ ★ ★ ★ ★

CHAPTER SEVEN

Partings

★ ★ ★ ★ ★ ★ ★ ★ ★ ★ ★ ★ ★ ★ ★

Julia and Ulysses were uncertain of what to do next. They put off thinking about it and went on vacation. It was no ordinary trip. Between May 1877 and September 1879, they circled the globe. Everywhere they went, they were treated as celebrities and entertained by royalty and heads of state. The entire tour was a progression of dinners and receptions given in their honor. Julia enjoyed it enormously.

They sailed for England, the first stop on their world tour, on May 17, 1877. Jesse, now nineteen, accompanied his parents. Julia took her maid. The group also included John Russell Young, a reporter for the *New*

★ ★ ★ ★ ★ ★ ★ ★ ★ ★ ★ ★ ★ ★ ★

The Grants sailed for England, the first stop on their world tour, on May 17, 1877.

Queen Victoria held a reception for the Grants at Windsor Castle.

Queen Victoria (1819–1901)

☆ ☆

Queen Victoria ruled England for an amazing sixty-four years. She and her husband, Prince Albert, had nine children. So many of her relatives became kings and queens in other countries that she was sometimes called the "grandmother of Europe." After Albert died in 1861, she spent many years in isolation and the rest of her life in mourning for him. Nevertheless, her reign was a time of great expansion and prosperity for England. The year before the Grants' visit, she had been proclaimed Empress of India. So widespread was her influence that most of the nineteenth century became known as the "Victorian Age."

York Herald. Young supplied the newspapers back home with details of the Grants' trip.

In England, the Grants were so deluged with invitations that they were able to spend only a few days with Nellie in her home near Southampton. Julia and Ulysses met the great statesman Benjamin Disraeli; poets Robert Browning and Matthew Arnold; and composer Arthur Sullivan. Queen Victoria invited them to a reception at Windsor Palace.

The Grants were entertained by the Duke of Wellington, son of the man who had defeated Napoleon at the Battle of Waterloo. Of the duke's palatial Apsley House, Julia wrote, "This great house was presented to Wellington by the government for the single victory at Waterloo, along with wealth and a noble title which will descend throughout his line. As I sat there, I thought, 'How would it have been if General Grant had been an Englishman—I wonder, I wonder?'"

The Grants visited France, Belgium, Italy, Germany, Switzerland, and Denmark. They cruised the Mediterranean aboard a U.S. Navy ship, visiting Naples and Pompeii. They also went to Egypt, where they took a steamer trip up the Nile River. Julia was awed by the pyramids and ruins but disturbed by the poverty of the people.

Julia enjoyed shopping for souvenirs and gifts for family and friends. Like many tourists, she made some purchases that she later regretted. In Egypt, she bought ostrich feathers, which she found to be "a perfect nuisance when I came home. They were not pretty and they needed finishing and I knew not where to send

The Grants and their son Jesse pose with the crew aboard the Vandalia *during their world tour.*

The Grants were impressed with the mighty Egyptian pyramids.

them. . . . Let me give a bit of advice here. Only buy what you need. You can get everything in New York better and cheaper than you can import it yourself."

In Palestine and Jerusalem, the Grants visited sites sacred to the Christian religion: the Holy Sepulchre, the tomb of Lazarus, and the Garden of Gethsemane.

The tour went on to Spain, Italy, and Holland. Jesse became homesick and sailed home. Fred arrived to take his place. Neither Julia nor Ulysses seemed to tire of traveling. Moving on to Asia, they visited India, China, Burma, Siam, Singapore, and Hong Kong. Julia marveled at the intelligence of the elephants working on the lumber plantations of Burma and admired the beauty of the Taj Mahal in India.

In China, General Grant and Julia were entertained by General Li Hung-chang.

The Grants and their party arriving in Japan, the last stop on their world tour

This glittering welcome-home reception for the Grants was held at San Francisco's Palace Hotel.

Japan was the last country on the tour. Ulysses wanted to see Australia, but Julia was ready to go home. They took a steamship across the Pacific and arrived in San Francisco. There, they were greeted by cheering crowds, and by their son Buck. By December of 1879, the Grants were back in Philadelphia.

Reversing his former stand, Grant now wanted the Republican nomination for president. Perhaps he could not imagine what else he could do.

Their son Buck greeted the Grants on their arrival.

James Garfield (1831–1881)

✭ ✭

The last president to be born in a log cabin, Garfield had been a professor of ancient languages and literature. He often amused his friends by writing Greek with one hand and Latin with the other, at the same time. During the Civil War, he showed his bravery at the Battle of Chickamauga by riding under heavy fire to deliver an important message to his general. Getting caught in the middle of things also led to his election to the presidency. At the 1880 Republican convention, three factions supported three different candidates, including Ulysses S. Grant. In a three-way tie, Garfield was nominated as a compromise candidate and went on to win the election. His presidential career was shortlived, however, for in July 1881 he became the second American president to be assassinated.

However, the nomination went to James A. Garfield, who won the election. Julia was bitterly disappointed.

Buck had started a Wall Street brokerage firm in partnership with Ferdinand Ward. He invited his father to join the firm. Although Ulysses knew little about finance, his contacts would bring business into the firm.

Wealthy friends had raised enough money on the Grants' behalf to buy them a mansion near Fifth Avenue in

William Henry Vanderbilt loaned a large sum of money to the firm of Grant & Ward.

New York City. The Grant mansion was decorated with souvenirs of the world tour. Julia loved life in New York City. She attended theaters, museums, and the opera and frequently saw her sons and their wives and children.

The Grants' prosperity ended in 1884. Ferdinand Ward had been making illegal money transactions. Ward, realizing that the firm of Grant & Ward was about to fail, asked Ulysses to raise $150,000 to keep the firm afloat. Ward claimed to need this money for only one day. Ulysses Grant called on a wealthy friend, William Vanderbilt, who immediately wrote a personal check for the large amount. Grant handed the check over to Ward, who promptly fled the country with the money.

Grant & Ward failed and the Grants were financially ruined. Once again, the name of Ulysses Grant was in the newspapers, associated with fraud and scandal. It was humiliating. Although it emerged that Grant had not known of the illegal dealings, he still owed Vanderbilt $150,000. The Grants repaid the loan with the deeds to various houses they owned. They kept only the houses in New York City and Long Branch, New Jersey.

A melancholy period followed. Money was scarce again. Ulysses began to write a series of magazine articles on the Civil War for *Century Magazine* in order to raise cash. Subscriptions to *Century* increased sharply when the articles appeared.

Mark Twain, the famous humorist and writer whose real name was

Mark Twain (1835–1910)

✳ ✳

Samuel Clemens lived a happy life as a steamboat pilot on the Mississippi River until the Civil War broke out. The fighting closed the river to steamboat traffic. Partly to avoid the war, Samuel accompanied his brother west and tried his hand at mining and prospecting. When these failed, he began to write for a newspaper, the Virginia City, Nevada, *Territorial Enterprise*. He took the pen name "Mark Twain," a riverboat term that meant the water was deep enough for a boat to pass. Twain became one of this country's greatest writers and humorists. Readers around the world still enjoy the adventures of his most famous young heroes, Huckleberry Finn and Tom Sawyer.

Samuel Clemens, had been a friend of the Grants for some years. Twain, who had become a publisher, offered Grant a book contract for his memoirs. The terms of the contract were so favorable that the Grants' financial problems would be solved once the book was published.

Finishing the book became a race against time. Ulysses Grant was dying. In October 1884, he was diagnosed with throat cancer. The disease was so far along that nothing could be done.

For a while, Julia refused to accept that Ulysses was dying. She was certain that this was a false alarm. "My

A very ill General Grant continued writing his memoirs every day, even though he was in great pain.

husband was healthy, temperate, strong. Why should he not be well and strong again? . . . I surely thought he would recover." Finally, she accepted the fact that his disease was fatal. In February 1885, she wrote to a friend, "Genl Grant is very, very ill. I cannot write how ill—my tears blind me."

Meanwhile, Grant was writing doggedly every day, despite his pain. He knew that if he could finish his book, Julia would be financially secure for the rest of her life.

In the summer of 1885, friends offered the Grants the use of a house in the Adirondack Mountains. Julia and Ulysses, accompanied by a nurse, a docter, a maid, and a valet, took a train to the summer home at Mount McGregor. Family members also gathered there. Fred and Jesse arrived with their wives and children. Nellie came from England to be with her parents.

Grant's last illness was a public affair, just as much of his life had been. The newspapers published reports on his health. Curious bystanders paraded past the cottage where Grant spent his last days.

Julia was with Ulysses constantly. She hid her sorrow and assumed a cheerful air.

The house at Mount McGregor, near Saratoga, New York, where Ulysses Grant spent his last days

Nellie (left), Fred (middle), Jesse (right), and other family members gathered at Mount McGregor to be with Ulysses during his last illness.

Ulysses Grant (center, in top hat), Julia (second from left, in striped skirt), and other family members pose for a photograph on the porch of the summer house in Mount McGregor.

This picture showing Ulysses S. Grant reading on the porch of the Mount McGregor house was taken on July 20, 1885, only three days before he died.

By mid-July, Grant had finished his book. His condition worsened immediately, and he died on the morning of July 23, 1885, at the age of sixty-three.

Julia had been strong for Grant's sake during his illness. After his death, she was overcome with grief. She remained in the cottage, seeing no one other than family members. She was too distraught to attend her husband's funeral in New York City on August 8. The pallbearers included Union generals Sherman and Sheridan and Confederate generals

Huge crowds gathered on Fifth Avenue in New York City as Grant's funeral procession passed.

Johnston and Buckner. Julia left Mount McGregor and returned to New York City.

Julia was grief-stricken for several years. She stayed at home much of the time, relying on her family for company and support. Fred and his family lived with her, so she was rarely alone until 1889, when Fred was sent to Vienna, Austria, as a diplomat. Julia later wrote, "With the general's death, fifteen years ago, I thought my life had been lived, for we had been inseparable. I saw nothing that could brighten or make interesting the remaining years. It was very dreary."

In 1894, she sold the New York City house and bought a mansion on Massachusetts Avenue in Washington, D.C. Nellie's marriage had ended in divorce, so Nellie and her three children moved in with Julia.

Julia was enjoying life once again. Money was not a problem because Grant's *Personal Memoirs* generated royalties of more than $400,000. Julia was a wealthy woman. As a former First Lady, she was treated with deference and respect. She still received visitors in her home one day each week, but was happiest in the company of her family and close friends. Julia took a great interest in the lives of her twelve grandchildren.

In 1896, General Li Hung-chang visited Julia. He had entertained the Grants when they were in China. He proudly presented Julia with the gift of a wheelchair and kept reminding her that they were both elderly. Julia managed to accept the unwelcome gift graciously. She was seventy years old and still strong and mobile.

Several years after Ulysses's death, Julia had started to write her own memoirs. The exercise of writing helped her to regain a purpose in life. When her memoirs were complete, she toyed with the idea of having them published. Since her husband's memoirs had provided such huge royalties, Julia thought her own memoirs would bring a nice price. She was disappointed at the amount of money publishers offered for her book. In addition, Julia feared that some people would be hurt or angered by the memoirs. She put the manuscript aside. It was not published until long after her death.

Julia Grant died at the age of seventy-six, seventeen years after the death of her husband.

Julia Grant died of heart failure on December 14, 1902, in her home in Washington, D.C. She was seventy-six years old. A week later, she was buried in Grant's Tomb, which overlooks the Hudson River, in New York City.

Dr. Frank Bristol, the minister of the Methodist Church that Julia attended in Washington, spoke of her at a memorial service, "She saw in him, the young lieutenant, power and greatness before anyone else. She

A week after her death, Julia Grant was buried with her husband in Grant's Tomb, overlooking the Hudson River in New York City.

helped to lift that genius from oblivion. He knew enough always to appreciate what his wife had done for him."

Julia had completed her own memoirs with a tribute to Ulysses, writing, "For nearly thirty-seven years, I, his wife, rested and was warmed in the sunlight of his loyal love and great fame, and now, even though his beautiful life has gone out, it is as when some far-off planet disappears from the heavens; the light of his glorious fame still reaches out to me, falls upon me, and warms me."

Profile of America, 1902: New Frontiers

☆ ☆ ☆ ☆ ☆ ☆ ☆ ☆ ☆ ☆ ☆ ☆ ☆ ☆ ☆ ☆ ☆ ☆ ☆

Julia Grant lived two years into an exciting new century. Americans felt optimistic and confident about their country and the future. "In the Good Old Summertime," a breezy song about summer fun, was the biggest hit of 1902. By this time, the Wild West was fading into memory. Frontiersmen were bygone heroes. Little was said about Native Americans, whose lands, lives, and dignity fell to white settlement. Popular books such as *The Virginian* romanticized the image of the cowboy. The land had been conquered. Now forty-five states strong, the United States looked to other frontiers.

More than 76 million people inhabited the country. People moved eagerly to the cities to find work in mills and factories. Women left small towns in droves hoping for a more exciting future in the big city. Immigrants came from Europe by the thousands searching for better lives. As everyone crowded into the cities, living conditions grew congested and difficult, especially for the poor, whose numbers increased daily. At the same time, the rich got richer. The country's largest corporation—United States Steel—had been born in 1901. A strike by 150,000 United Mine Workers against Pennsylvania coal mines pointed up the distress caused by the wide gap between the rich and the poor.

For Americans in between, the modern age was in full swing. Twenty-three thousand people owned automobiles. Rayon, the first successful synthetic textile, was patented. In the first post-season football game, Michigan beat Stanford 49–0 at the Tournament of Roses. President Teddy Roosevelt, a strapping outdoorsman, inspired a rage for outdoor recreation and living, and the government began to establish public parks.

Had Julia Grant lived another year, she would have witnessed the first manned, motored flight made by the Wright brothers at Kitty Hawk, North Carolina. New frontiers, indeed.

Presidents and Their First Ladies

President	Birth–Death	First Lady	Birth–Death
1789–1797			
George Washington	1732–1799	Martha Dandridge Custis Washington	1731–1802
1797–1801			
John Adams	1735–1826	Abigail Smith Adams	1744–1818
1801–1809			
Thomas Jefferson†	1743–1826		
1809–1817			
James Madison	1751–1836	Dolley Payne Todd Madison	1768–1849
1817–1825			
James Monroe	1758–1831	Elizabeth Kortright Monroe	1768–1830
1825–1829			
John Quincy Adams	1767–1848	Louisa Catherine Johnson Adams	1775–1852
1829–1837			
Andrew Jackson†	1767–1845	Rachel Donelson Jackson	1767–1828
1837–1841			
Martin Van Buren†	1782–1862		
1841			
William Henry Harrison‡	1773–1841		
1841–1845			
John Tyler	1790–1862	Letitia Christian Tyler (1841–1842)	1790–1842
		Julia Gardiner Tyler (1844–1845)	1820–1889
1845–1849			
James K. Polk	1795–1849	Sarah Childress Polk	1803–1891
1849–1850			
Zachary Taylor	1784–1850	Margaret Mackall Smith Taylor	1788–1852
1850–1853			
Millard Fillmore	1800–1874	Abigail Powers Fillmore	1798–1853
1853–1857			
Franklin Pierce	1804–1869	Jane Means Appleton Pierce	1806–1863
1857–1861			
James Buchanan*	1791–1868		
1861–1865			
Abraham Lincoln	1809–1865	Mary Todd Lincoln	1818–1882
1865–1869			
Andrew Johnson	1808–1875	Eliza McCardle Johnson	1810–1876
1869–1877			
Ulysses S. Grant	1822–1885	Julia Dent Grant	1826–1902
1877–1881			
Rutherford B. Hayes	1822–1893	Lucy Ware Webb Hayes	1831–1889
1881			
James A. Garfield	1831–1881	Lucretia Rudolph Garfield	1832–1918
1881–1885			
Chester A. Arthur†	1829–1886		

† wife died before he took office ‡ wife too ill to accompany him to Washington * never married

1885–1889			
Grover Cleveland	1837–1908	Frances Folsom Cleveland	1864–1947
1889–1893			
Benjamin Harrison	1833–1901	Caroline Lavinia Scott Harrison	1832–1892
1893–1897			
Grover Cleveland	1837–1908	Frances Folsom Cleveland	1864–1947
1897–1901			
William McKinley	1843–1901	Ida Saxton McKinley	1847–1907
1901–1909			
Theodore Roosevelt	1858–1919	Edith Kermit Carow Roosevelt	1861–1948
1909–1913			
William Howard Taft	1857–1930	Helen Herron Taft	1861–1943
1913–1921			
Woodrow Wilson	1856–1924	Ellen Louise Axson Wilson (1913–1914)	1860–1914
		Edith Bolling Galt Wilson (1915–1921)	1872–1961
1921–1923			
Warren G. Harding	1865–1923	Florence Kling Harding	1860–1924
1923–1929			
Calvin Coolidge	1872–1933	Grace Anna Goodhue Coolidge	1879–1957
1929–1933			
Herbert Hoover	1874–1964	Lou Henry Hoover	1874–1944
1933–1945			
Franklin D. Roosevelt	1882–1945	Anna Eleanor Roosevelt	1884–1962
1945–1953			
Harry S. Truman	1884–1972	Elizabeth Virginia Wallace Truman	1885–1982
1953–1961			
Dwight D. Eisenhower	1890–1969	Mamie Geneva Doud Eisenhower	1896–1979
1961–1963			
John F. Kennedy	1917–1963	Jacqueline Bouvier Kennedy Onassis	1929–1994
1963–1969			
Lyndon B. Johnson	1908–1973	Claudia Taylor (Lady Bird) Johnson	1912–
1969–1974			
Richard Nixon	1913–1994	Patricia Ryan Nixon	1912–1993
1974–1977			
Gerald Ford	1913–	Elizabeth Bloomer Ford	1918–
1977–1981			
James Carter	1924–	Rosalynn Smith Carter	1927–
1981–1989			
Ronald Reagan	1911–	Nancy Davis Reagan	1923–
1989–1993			
George Bush	1924–	Barbara Pierce Bush	1925–
1993–			
William Jefferson Clinton	1946–	Hillary Rodham Clinton	1947–

Julia Dent Grant Timeline

1822	★	Ulysses S. Grant is born
1825	★	John Quincy Adams becomes president after a disputed election
		Erie Canal opens, connecting New York City to cities on the Great Lakes
1826	★	Julia Dent Grant is born on January 26
1828	★	Andrew Jackson is elected president
1829	★	*Encyclopedia Americana*, the first U.S. encyclopedia, is published
		Englishman James Smithson leaves money to found the Smithsonian Institution in Washington, D.C.
1830	★	U.S. population is 12,866,020
1832	★	Andrew Jackson is reelected president
1833	★	Oberlin College becomes the first college to admit women
1836	★	Martin Van Buren is elected president
1837	★	The United States suffers an economic depression
1840	★	U.S. population is 17,069,453
		William Henry Harrison is elected president
1841	★	William Henry Harrison dies a month after taking office
		John Tyler becomes president
1842	★	Ulysses S. Grant graduates from the U.S. Military Academy at West Point
1844	★	James Polk is elected president
1846	★	United States declares war on Mexico and Ulysses S. Grant takes part in several battles

1847	★	Lieutenant Ulysses S. Grant is part of U.S. Army that captures Mexico City
1848	★	Treaty of Guadalupe Hidalgo ends the Mexican War and gives most of the present-day Southwest to the United States
		Julia Dent marries Ulysses S. Grant
		First U.S. women's rights meeting is held in Seneca Falls, New York
		Zachary Taylor is elected president
1849	★	Elizabeth Blackwell becomes the first woman in the world to receive a medical degree
1850	★	Julia Dent Grant's first child, Frederick, is born
		U.S. population is 23,191,876
		Zachary Taylor dies and Millard Fillmore becomes president
1852	★	Julia Dent Grant's second child, Ulysses Simpson, Jr. (Buck), is born
		Franklin Pierce is elected president
		Harriet Beecher Stowe's *Uncle Tom's Cabin* is published, increasing antislavery feelings in the United States
1854	★	Republican Party is formed and calls for the abolition of slavery
		Ulysses S. Grant resigns from the army and moves his family to a farm near St. Louis, Missouri
1855	★	Julia Dent Grant's third child, Ellen (Nellie), is born
1856	★	James Buchanan is elected president
1858	★	Julia Dent's fourth child, Jesse, is born
		The Grants move to St. Louis
1860	★	U.S. population is 31,443,321
		Abraham Lincoln is elected president
		The Grants move to Galena, Illinois
1861	★	Confederate States of America (eleven seceded Southern states) is formed
		The Civil War begins
		Ulysses S. Grant is made a colonel and leaves Galena to fight in the Civil War

1863	★	President Lincoln issues the Emancipation Proclamation
		Confederate army is defeated at Gettysburg
		General Grant wins a major Union victory at Vicksburg
		President Lincoln gives the Gettysburg Address
1864	★	**President Lincoln appoints Grant general-in-chief of all the Union armies**
		Abraham Lincoln is reelected president
1865	★	Robert E. Lee surrenders the Confederate army to Grant at Appomattox Court House
		Abraham Lincoln is assassinated
		Andrew Johnson becomes president
		Thirteenth Amendment, which outlaws slavery in the United States, is added to the U.S. Constitution
1867	★	**Congress passes Reconstruction Acts that put the Southern states under military control**
1868	★	President Andrew Johnson is impeached by the U.S. House of Representatives but is acquitted by the U.S. Senate
		Fourteenth Amendment is added to the Constitution
		Ulysses S. Grant is elected president
1869	★	**First U.S. transcontinental railroad is completed**
1870	★	U.S. population is 39,818,449
		Fifteenth Amendment is added to the Constitution, giving African American males the right to vote
1872	★	**Ulysses S. Grant is reelected president**
		Yellowstone National Park, the nation's first, is established
1873	★	Panic of 1873 sets off a five-year depression
1875	★	**Congress passes Civil Rights Act, which guarantees African Americans equal rights in public places**
1876	★	George Armstrong Custer and his troops are killed at the Battle of the Little Bighorn
		Alexander Graham Bell successfully tests the telephone

1877	★	Rutherford B. Hayes becomes president
		Julia and Ulysses S. Grant begin a world tour
		Reconstruction ends when last U.S. troops leave the South
1879	★	Julia and Ulysses Grant return to the United States from their world tour
1880	★	U.S. population is 50,155,783
		James Garfield is elected president
1881	★	James A. Garfield is shot and dies ninety days later
		Chester A. Arthur becomes president
		The Grants move to New York City
1882	★	Congress approves a pension for all widows of U.S. presidents
1883	★	Civil Rights Act of 1875 is repealed by the Supreme Court
1884	★	Grover Cleveland is elected president
		Ulysses S. Grant is diagnosed with throat cancer and begins writing his memoirs
1885	★	Ulysses S. Grant finishes writing his memoirs
		Ulysses S. Grant dies
1886	★	Statue of Liberty, a gift from France, is dedicated
1888	★	Benjamin Harrison is elected president
1890	★	U.S. population is 62,947,714
1892	★	Grover Cleveland is elected president
1894	★	Julia Grant moves to Washington, D.C.
1896	★	William McKinley is elected president
1900	★	U.S. population is 75,994,575
		William McKinley is reelected president
1901	★	First Rose Bowl game is held
		William McKinley is assassinated
		Theodore Roosevelt becomes president
1902	★	Julia Dent Grant dies on December 14

Fast Facts about Julia Dent Grant

Born: January 26, 1826, at White Haven farm outside St. Louis, Missouri

Died: December 14, 1902, in Washington, D.C.

Burial Site: Grant's Tomb in New York City

Parents: Frederick Dent and Ellen Bray Wrenshall Dent

Education: One-room school until age ten; boarding school in St. Louis until age seventeen

Marriage: To Ulysses S. Grant on August 22, 1848, until his death in 1885

Children: Frederick, Ulysses Simpson (Buck), Ellen (Nellie), and Jesse

Places She Lived: White Haven, St. Louis, and Hardscrabble in Missouri (1826–1860); Galena, Illinois (1860–1865); Washington, D.C. (1866–1877, 1894–1902); New York City (1881–1894); brief periods in Burlington and Long Branch, New Jersey, and in Philadelphia, Pennsylvania

Major Achievements:

* Gained admiration and respect from General Grant's staff for visiting his headquarters and caring for wounded soldiers in field hospitals during the Civil War
* Renovated and redecorated the White House with rich furniture, carpets, and glittering chandeliers
* Improved the appearance of White House staff members by having them wear gloves and uniforms and enriched the quality of White House meals by hiring an Italian chef
* With the assistance of wives of Cabinet members, held a weekly reception in the Blue Room which was open to the public
* With the president, hosted large weekly dinner parties that had as many as thirty courses
* Planned the wedding of her daughter Nellie to Algernon Charles Frederic Sartoris, which was held in the East Room
* Was the first former First Lady to travel around the world (1877–1879)
* Wrote her memoirs, which were finally published in 1975, seventy-three years after her death

Fast Facts about
Ulysses S. Grant's Presidency

Terms of Office: Elected in 1868 and reelected in 1872; served as the eighteenth president of the United States from 1869 to 1877

Vice Presidents: Schuyler Colfax (1869–1873) and Henry Wilson (1873–1875)

Major Policy Decisions and Legislation:

* Supported ratification of the Fifteenth Amendment, which extended the right to vote to African American men
* Signed the act establishing Yellowstone National Park in 1872
* Appointed a commission in 1872 to study the possibility of building the Panama Canal
* Signed a civil rights act in 1875 that gave African Americans equal rights in public places

Major Events:

* The first transcontinental railroad in the United States was completed at Promontory, Utah, in 1869
* The Crédit Mobilier scandal, uncovered in 1872, showed that both of Grant's vice presidents had accepted bribes, while they were members of Congress, to take profits from the construction of the transcontinental railroad
* The Panic of 1873 began when a major New York bank failed, causing a depression that lasted until 1878
* The Whiskey Ring scandal was uncovered in 1875 in which Grant's personal secretary Orville Babcock and other officials were charged with taking bribes from liquor distillers so the distillers would avoid paying taxes
* William Belknap, Grant's secretary of war, resigned on March 2, 1876, after the House of Representatives impeached him for illegally making profits from Indian lands under his control
* General George Armstrong Custer was defeated by Native Americans at the Battle of the Little Bighorn on June 25, 1876
* Colorado was admitted as the thirty-eighth state on August 1, 1876

Where to Visit

Appomattox Court House National Historical Park
P.O. Box 218
Appomattox, Virginia 24522
(804) 352-8987

Grant's Tomb
Riverside Drive and 122nd Street
New York, New York 10003

Shiloh National Military Park
Route 1, Box 9
Shiloh, Tennessee 38376

U. S. Grant Birthplace
1591 State Route 232
Point Pleasant, Ohio 45153
(937) 553-4911

Ulysses S. Grant Home State Historic Site
500 Bouthillier Street
Galena, Illinois 61036
(815) 777-3310

Ulysses S. Grant National Historic Site
7400 Grant Road
St. Louis, Missouri 63123-1801
(314) 842-3298

United States Military Academy
West Point, New York 10996
(914) 938-2638

Vicksburg National Military Park
3201 Clay Street
Vicksburg, Mississippi 39180

Online Sites of Interest

The First Ladies of the United States of America
http://www2.whitehouse.gov/WH/glimpse/firstladies/html/firstladies.html
A portrait and biographical sketch of each First Lady plus links to other White House sites

Fort Donelson National Battlefield
http://www.nps.gov/fodo/
Information about the first major battle of the Civil War won by the Union. Includes visitor information and a link to the National Park Service Home Page.

Shiloh National Military Park
http://www.nps.gov/shil/
Information about the bloody Civil War battle in Tennessee that was the decisive victory for the Union. Includes visitor information and a link to the National Park Service Home Page.

The Ulysses S. Grant Association
http://www.lib.siu.edu/projects/usgrant/
Information about the association that has collected and published thousands of Grant documents. Includes a U. S. Grant chronology, a list of the Grant papers published so far, plus *The Personal Memoirs of Julia Dent Grant* and more.

Ulysses S. Grant, a Guide for Students
http://www.css.edu/mkelsey/student.html
Information on Grant plus links to many websites with Grant information and photos, including books for students and the U. S. Grant Network Home Page at *http://www.css.edu/mkelsey/gppg.html*

Vicksburg National Military Park
http://www.nps.gov/vick/
Information on the Civil War battle and siege of Vicksburg, Mississippi. Includes visitor information and a link to the National Park Service Home Page.

The White House
http://www.whitehouse.gov/WH/Welcome.html
Information about the current president and vice president; White House history and tours; biographies of past presidents and their families; a virtual White House library; current events, and much more.

The White House for Kids
http://www.whitehouse.gov/WH/kids/html/kidshome.html
Includes information about White House kids, past and present; famous "First Pets," past and present; historic moments of the presidency; and much more.

For Further Reading

Fleming, Alice Mulcahey. *General's Lady: The Life of Julia Grant*. Philadelphia: Lippincott, 1971.

Gould, Lewis L. (ed). *American First Ladies: Their Lives and Their Legacy*. New York: Garland Publishing, 1996.

Kent, Zachary. *The Story of the Battle of Shiloh*. Cornerstones of Freedom series. Chicago: Childrens Press, 1991.

————. *Ulysses S. Grant: Eighteenth President of the United States*. Encyclopedia of Presidents series. Chicago: Childrens Press, 1989.

Klapthor, Margaret Brown. *The First Ladies*. Washington, D.C.: White House Historical Association in cooperation with the National Geographic Society, 1994.

Lindsey, Rae. *The Presidents' First Ladies*. New York: Franklin Watts, 1989.

Mayo, Edith P. (ed.). *The Smithsonian Book of the First Ladies: Their Lives, Times, and Issues*. New York: Henry Holt, 1996.

Nardo, Don. *The Mexican–American War*. San Diego: Lucent Books, 1991.

O'Brien, Steven. *Ulysses S. Grant*. World Leaders Past and Present series. New York: Chelsea House Publishers, 1991.

Index

Page numbers in **boldface type** indicate illustrations

Photo Identifications

Cover: Julia Dent Grant

Page 8: The Grant family (left to right: Julia, Frederick, Ellen [Nellie], Ulysses S., Ulysses S., Jr. [Buck], and Jesse)

Page 16: Portrait of Julia by Martha Harriett Hoke

Page 26: Julia Dent Grant at the beginning of the Civil War

Page 34: General Ulysses S. Grant and his wife, Julia Dent Grant, about 1862–1864

Page 46: Ulysses, Fred, and Julia at City Point toward the end of the Civil War

Page 58: The official White House portrait of Julia Dent Grant, a photograph by Matthew Brady

Page 76: A photograph of Julia Dent Grant taken in the 1880s

Photo Credits©

The Galena/Jo Daviess County Historical Society—Cover, 11, 14, 58, 96 (bottom)

Archive Photos—8, 45 (top), 84; Kean Archive, 45 (bottom), 85, 90 , 97 (bottom and second from top)

Stock Montage, Inc.—10, 22 (bottom), 28, 32, 33, 39, 55, 60 (bottom), 69, 78 (bottom), 80, 81, 88 (bottom left and bottom right), 93, 99 (bottom)

Corbis–Bettmann—12, 20, 31, 40, 43, 46, 48, 52, 53, 54 (both pictures), 67 (right), 72, 82 (both pictures), 86, 87, 88 (top), 89, 97 (top), 98 (top), 99 (middle)

North Wind Picture Archives—13, 19, 60 (top), 64 (top), 66, 67 (left), 74, 78 (top), 83 (bottom), 88 (bottom middle)

Lloyd Ostendorf—15

Courtesy of Chicago Historical Society—16, 37, 68, 96 (top)

Ohio Historical Society—22 (top), 26, 34, 76

AP/Wide World Photos—23, 30, 97 (second from bottom)

UPI/Corbis–Bettmann—38, 65, 91, 94

Historical Society of Washington, D.C.—44

North Wind Pictures—49, 51, 83 (top)

White House Historical Association— 50, 58, 61, 64 (bottom right), 98 (bottom)

Rutherford B. Hayes Presidential Center, Fremont, Ohio—62

Smithsonian Institution—64 (bottom left)

SuperStock International, Inc.—71, 75; National Portrait Gallery, 79, 99 (top)

About the Author

Christine Fitz-Gerald holds a B.A. in English literature from Ohio University and a Masters in Management from Northwestern University. She has been employed by the Quaker Oats Company, General Mills, and Honeywell, Inc. She now resides in Wilmette, Illinois, with her husband and three children. Her Children's Press titles include *James Monroe* and *William Henry Harrison* in the Encyclopedia of Presidents series, and *Meriwether Lewis and William Clark* in the World's Great Explorers series.